USING
Big Books and
Predictable Books

PRISCILLA LYNCH

SCHOLASTIC

Toronto • Sydney • New York • London • Auckland

To Adrian Peetoom

in gratitude for so many years of productive arguments

Scholastic Inc.
730 Broadway, New York, NY 10003, USA
Scholastic Canada Ltd.
123 Newkirk Road, Richmond Hill, Ontario, Canada L4C 3G5
Ashton Scholastic Limited
Private Bag 1, Penrose, Auckland, New Zealand
Ashton Scholastic Pty Limited
P.O. Box 579, Gosford, NSW 2250, Australia
Scholastic Publications Ltd.
Holly Walk, Leamington Spa, Warwickshire CV32 4LS, England

ISBN 0-590-71368-X

Canadian Cataloguing in Publication Data

Lynch, Priscilla
  Using big books and predictable books

Edited by Adrian Peetoom.
Includes bibliographies.
ISBN 0-590-71368-X

1. Reading (Primary). I Peetoom, Adrian.
II. Title

LB1573.33.L95 1986   372.4   C87-007954-9

109   Printed in Canada   1 2 3 4/9

Introduction

In recent years we have come to realize the importance of real books as part of our curriculum, *quality* real books. We have also learned that:

- Big Books enable children to learn to read quickly.
- Predictable books ensure successful reading experiences.
- Early successful reading creates confidence in beginners.
- Excited, enthusiastic responses to reading make teaching more enjoyable.

Teachers have questions about "what" and "how," about organization of space and time, about what to do when, and how much of it. Two persistent questions are:

1. What's the best way to use Big Books?
2. What can be done with predictable books?

There is no one "best way" to teach, any more than there is one "best way" to learn. We all have our different styles. We all look for help, adapt what we find, and apply it to our classrooms in our own way, just as children watch, listen, absorb and use our demonstrations in their own way. This guide contains *suggestions* intended mainly for teachers who have never used, or are just beginning to use Big Books and predictable books as integral parts of their language arts programs. For teachers who have already refined Whole Language teaching strategies, there are more specific resources, such as the *Whole Language Sourcebook* (Scholastic, 1986), by two Nova Scotia classroom teachers, Jane Baskwill and Paulette Whitman.

Also included (see pages 15-17) are practical suggestions for advance planning.

What to do with Big Books

Big Books are designed to be shared by a group, usually up to eight children. When children hear a story all the way through, and enjoy it, they are learning the *purpose* of reading. When they read together in a shared, invitational way, they are assured that they will be able to read that book for themselves later on. They are immersed in natural, memorable language with high-impact, meaningful stories they will treasure the rest of their lives.

The first day

Show your children the cover of the Big Book. Ask them, "What do you see?" and list their responses on the chalkboard or chart paper, with their initials after each contribution.

> The first letters most children want to learn to make and to read are the letters of their names. Putting their initials next to their observations reinforces the idea that their personal thoughts can be written down and saved, and also gives them practice in locating and naming letters. You are drawing their attention to the formation of words that "stand for" their thoughts. You are saving their thoughts in writing so they can be recovered and re-examined as you read the book together.

Talk about what a book is. Point out the author and illustrator, and even the publisher, the copyright, and the dedication.

> Discussion of what they see on the cover activates their prior knowledge. You are modeling what they will soon do in their own independent reading.

Ask a second question: "What do you think the story may be about?" Again write their suggestions on the chalkboard, with their initials.

> This question activates further prior knowledge. You are helping your children do some collaborative learning, gathering and using information from each other. You are showing them that they have lots of personal knowledge to bring to a story and that

reading is transactional. Reading demands not only the author's words in print, but also the reader's own world knowledge. Together the author and the reader produce an interpretation of the story. You are also encouraging children to predict without fear of failure.

As you and your children become more familiar with the routine, ask them, "What questions do you think will be answered in the story?" Record those ideas too.

Now their predictions are extended to the actual substance of the story. The more you can show them that what they *already have in their heads* can make reading easy and pleasurable, the more confident they will become. This takes time, but it is time well spent. You are getting them into the habit of predicting and confirming, the cornerstones of real reading.

Depending on your children, this may be enough discussion for the first day.

Note: Leave the children's thoughts on the board. As the book is read, their predictions and suggestions will receive confirmation, which will build their confidence.

The second day

Now you are ready to read the Big Book aloud to the group. Please read it with enthusiasm. Close your door if you have to, but convey the full impact of the story dramatically. Use your voice to emphasize the predictable parts of the story, the repetitions, the rhymes, and the colorful sounds of some words. Your delight in the book is infectious.

Do *not* pause for their questions or comments during this first reading. You want them to hear the whole story, without interruption, so they get the sense of its deep structure, and have the information they need to confirm their predictions immediately.

After you've read the book all the way through, turn to the children's original suggestions, saved on the chalkboard or chart paper.

Ask them to find their own initials and to read (with your help if necessary) their comments and predictions.

How many of their ideas appeared in the story? This is the time for lots of praise, because there are sure to be matches between their ideas and the ideas in the book.

Give the children time to express their reactions to the book.

They will have opinions about everything that happened in the story, and since they'll be anxious to express those ideas, give them full opportunity. Recap the story with them. Note what happened first, next and last. What part did they like best? What illustrations did they especially like? Did something similar ever happen to them?

Go through the same process with your other groups. Don't skimp, even if what you did with your first group has been listened to "extra-curricularly." Listening will help the other children internalize the deep structure of the story long before they get to the surface structure, the actual print.

The third day

Go back and read the Big Book again with each group, but this time tell the children that you want their questions and comments on *every* page as you are reading. You'll stop to listen to each opinion and question, and you'll give them time to examine the pictures more closely. Read a page and then wait for them to talk about it with you.

Language is social. It is used to question, to explain, to express an opinion, to control what others are saying and doing, and to create a genuine cooperative learning group. The more the children talk about the book, the more they are using the words in the book, making that vocabulary their own. The more they question the information or events in the book, the more they are clarifying their own thoughts and recreating the author's phrases and concepts. The more they hear the book with your intonation carrying the meaning, the more they will be able to remember how the story "works." The more they hear and see the story, the more they will use what they've absorbed in their own writing.

When questions arise, ask the rest of the group to suggest answers. Your children may find that some of their ideas about the story differ from those of others in the group. You are making it possible for them to check their interpretations against others.

This process is sometimes called "intersubjective analysis" and it is a very important part of any reading experience. Discussion also gives children a high shared content to work with. Shared content means that each child knows the words and concepts every other child in the group is using. This is particularly important for ESL children, because the high shared content permits them to use common phrases again and again, modeling their phrasing and intonations after your reading and their friends' comments.

Don't rush this page-by-page discussion. When one child makes a comment and another disagrees, take them back to the print, rereading and rehearing for clarification. Be receptive to divergent thinking, entertaining all of their ideas seriously and thoughtfully.

Every story is a jumping-off place. What memories does it awaken? What questions does it prompt? What ideas emerge? What other books have the same problem?

In-depth discussion demonstrates to the children that print doesn't change from reading to reading, that they can refer back and reprocess print any time they are confused about something, and that differences of opinion are not unusual, but the norm. It also encourages them to link what is happening in the story to events in their own lives. You should not be primarily concerned with *what the book says*, but with *what it says to the children*. The important learning comes from the interaction between the author's words and the children's personal knowledge.

As you read each page, listen and watch the children, as always.

How much of the story do they understand? How easily and clearly do they express their thoughts? How many words do they recognize on the page? How do they interpret the illustrations? How willing are they to join in the discussion? How much experience do they bring to the story?

Do the same with each group. Chances are very good that while you work with the others your first group will want to draw a picture of something that links to the story, or write a bit about some remembered personal experience, using "invented" (also called "utilitarian" or "pragmatic") spelling.

The fourth day

Tell your children you are going to read the Big Book all the way through again, without stopping. This time invite them to join in whenever they think they remember part of the story.

This is their opportunity to role-play themselves as successful readers. No one fails. If they make a miscue, they can self-correct without embarrassment. There is no failure attached to invitational, shared reading. The object of the exercise is to heighten their enjoyment of the book, and of their reading expcerience. Each child supports every other child, and you support all of them. Some children will remember more of the plot than others. Some will remember the predictable, repetitive segments more quickly than others. Children grow at different rates, and they learn at different rates. The important thing is that they are all enjoying the book, that they are attending to your voice and to the print as much as they can, and that they are perceiving themselves as competent readers.

Often children will join in at *exactly* the same time as you read. (Or even ahead of you!) Ask, "How did you know that word was coming up next?" to see what clues they are using to know what to say.

Did some predict the whole story and therefore know when the phrases would appear? Did some get clues from the page itself, from the illustration or the organization of the print? Did some actually recognize a word on the page, from the first letter or configuration? You will discover they use all sorts of clues, and the class will benefit from hearing them. In this way you are introducing them to some of the strategies they have already developed, and you are encouraging them to think about their own thinking (metacognition).

After the children have had a chance to explain how they knew what was coming next, read the story aloud again. Invite them all to join in once more.

This gives the whole group a second opportunity to enjoy the story, plus a chance to *consciously* use some of the clues that have been talked about.

When they have shared the story again, ask them what phrases or sentences they remember. Write those on the chalkboard, saying each word as you write it. Then ask one child, someone you *know* can remember, to read them aloud with you. Ask the others to join in as you go through the phrases a second time. Run your finger (or a pointer) under each word as it is said aloud, and leave clear spaces (sound spaces and board spaces) between each word.

You are asking your children to "eye/voice point." Some may not yet be certain what a "word" is. Put your hands around words as they say them, and draw their attention to the space between words. They need lots of practice in "matching."

Transfer those phrases to a large piece of chart paper so they will be available for reference when the children want to write their own stories. One copy will serve all groups, but make sure that the next groups all go through the procedure on the board first.

The fifth day

Read the book aloud again.

Children do not tire of these books. You may, but they won't. They are acting the part of successful readers, and that is a very satisfying experience. They know the story. They can predict how it will end, and they are right every time!

During this reading, do some *oral cloze*. When you come to a part you think most will remember, pause and let the children "fill in" the words for you.

Some will fill in from memory, but some will actually be focusing on the page, following your finger or a pointer as you run it underneath the words. (Your pointer also reinforces the fact that the story comes from the print, not from the illustrations.) You have gone over the book enough times to be sure they'll remember the phrases as you stop to wait for their fill-ins. Again, since you are inviting them to read aloud *together*, even the child who can't remember all the phrases exactly doesn't fail, because he or she has the support of the shared reading group. Oral cloze also reinforces the sample/predict/confirm-or-correct pattern.

Teach your children the strategy of "rerun." If what they fill in does not make sense when they hear it, a "red light" should go on in their heads that says, "Stop and go back over what you've read." All print should make sense and sound like English. If it doesn't, there's a miscue someplace and it needs fixing.

This is what the children did when they learned to talk. They already know that in talking they must make sense, that what they say must sound right, because if it doesn't, nobody will understand them. And they do want to be understood when they speak.

So you are making use of what they already know how to do: check for meaning. When they join in with your voice, they are listening to their own voices. If what they are saying doesn't sound right or make sense, they can rerun the sentence, go back over it to locate the problem. As you teach them to do this, most of them will be rerunning from memory at first. Later on they will check each word. The habit of rerunning is a vital one. They will use it again and again as independent readers.

Next (or the following day) put one or two sentences from the book on the board and delete one word, drawing a line where the word would go. This is *written cloze*, and it is introduced *after* oral cloze. Run your finger (or pointer) under the sentence and read each word, using the word "something" as a placeholder for a deletion. Ask, "Can anyone think of a word that might go in this sentence so it makes sense?" When a child has made a prediction, from the book or from personal experience, write the word on the line. Go back over the sentence, rerunning it aloud, using the predicted word. Ask, "Does that make sense?" and "Does that sound like English?" Encourage the children to rerun the sentence aloud for themselves to check their prediction. Ask if anyone can think of another prediction that might go in that sentence, and go through the same process.

Because this is such an important activity, take time to do it over and over again until the children come to see rerunning as a useful confirming technique. Checking for meaning is their most important strategy, and rerunning is a good way to do that. You are also proving to them once again how much they already know in their own heads, how much they bring to print, and how much they can trust print to be sensible and meaningful.

Oral and written cloze represent the way good readers read: sampling just enough of the print to make a prediction about what's coming next in the sentence and then reading on to confirm their predictions. They do not read every letter of every word, nor every word of every sentence. They use only what is needed of the graphic information, plus their own personal knowledge, to make sense out of print. They negotiate meaning with the author.

Oral and written cloze exercises help children get into the habit of reading *through* an unknown word, reading through to the end of the sentence, and sometimes through to the end of the *next* sentence, looking for more information. Big Books draw their attention to the redundancies in language, to the predictable elements in print, and to the cueing systems found in English. Most Big Books contain rich, *memorable* language that confirms what children already know about how language works. Most children come to school recognizing the signs and phrases they see around them. They have already mastered the syntax of a very complex language. They *expect* language to make sense and Big Books and predictable books contain language that *does* make sense.

It is much easier for children to learn to read when they can count on the stories to be meaningful and full of interesting words and concepts. It is much easier for them to remember the deep structure of a plot if that plot moves quickly and has dramatic events in it, plus a satisfying ending. When sentences are meaningful and memorable, children can quickly make the words "fit" (eye/voice match) as they read them. Conversely, they will recognize when they have "read" the sentence and have *not* matched up the words correctly, having too many or too few words left at the end.

The sixth day

Introduce a new Big Book at this point, if your children are ready for it, and go through the first day's routine. After that, return to the already heard story for more cloze exercises and practice with letter/sound correspondences.

Many teachers find the small note pads with gummed edges very useful for cloze reading. They come in a variety of sizes, to cover letters, words or phrases so the children can make "educated guesses" about the hidden elements.

Tell the children you've covered up some letters and words as a guessing game for them. As you and they read the story aloud together, encourage them to guess what word or words are under the notepaper. When they have guessed, one child can come to the book and lift up the gummed paper to see if they are right. Remind them to rerun the sentence to look for meaning, and to read through the next sentence to confirm their meaning. Again ask them how they knew what the covered-up words might be.

Their responses will serve to remind them of *what they already do* when they are looking for meaning. They ask themselves, "Does this make sense?" (the semantic strategy) and, "Does this sound like English?" (the syntactic strategy). As you introduce the letters in their names and the letter/sound correspondences, you will be giving them a third strategy, the graphophonic strategy.

At this point, some of your children may be "staying with the print" in this familiar book, actually trying to read exactly what is on the page, word by word. Others in the group may still be "saying" the story without focusing on the individual words or word clusters. This mix of reading behaviors is to be expected.

Some children will need lots of read-aloud practice before they begin to use the graphophonic strategy you're teaching them. Others will move in and out of the "saying" mode to the "reading" mode, practicing the semantic and syntactic strategies *along with* the graphophonic strategy, trying to determine how much of each strategy they need to use to predict sensibly.

Children who are still "saying" the story will read quickly and with expression, modeling what you have demonstrated. When students begin to focus on each word, using the graphic information on the page to say the words, they slow down considerably. They are looking at the initial letters and the configuration of words to get the meaning. They are putting their other two strategies on hold *temporarily* while they figure out this new strategy, the graphophonic one. Their reading behavior becomes halting and hesitant. Ironically, the hesitations are a sign of solid progress. Your readers are now exploring alternative strategies and need time to practice until they internalize the procedures.

Spend time with the letter forms and the names of the letter forms, using the Big Book they have *already read*.

Helping the children to identify and name the beginning letters in their own names will now help them to associate other initial letters and sounds. Teaching letter forms is always done using *known material*, going from the sound of the word to its visual representation.

Concentrating on graphophonic information means concentrating on the *mechanics* of print. When your children are concentrating on mechanics, you don't want them struggling with meaning at the same time. They already *know* the meaning of the sentences in the Big Book they've read with you. Now they are able to focus their attention on initial letters and letter/sound associations without struggling with meaning too. If they are having trouble with a particular initial letter, they can always go back and rerun the known sentence to get semantic and syntactic help. You are convincing them that they do not have to rely on just one strategy to make sense of print. They have at least *three* strategies on hand. Always identify those strategies as they are using them so they develop an awareness of control over them.

Have the children identify and name the letters you are teaching. For instance, they can find all the *g*'s on a page by pointing to them, tracing them, or saying the words that have *g* as an initial letter. Tell them that you are going to say a word that begins with the letter *g* in print. Say the word and then see if someone can find it on the page. Point to the found word, say it, and ask if someone will find the letter *g* in that word. One child points to the word, says it, and then points specifically to the letter *g*. The child repeats the word and says that it begins with the letter *g*.

This is not decontextualizing either the letters or the words. You are not isolating the sound associated with that letter, nor are you presenting a word in isolation. You *are* giving your children a known context for figuring out sound/symbol correspondences. They are matching the name of the letter with the form of the letter, and they are associating the sound of the word with the printed form of the word. You are setting them up for success rather than failure.

Keep your groups flexible.

Some children will be ready to go on to more letter/sound associations while others still need some additional story reading without the graphophonic strategy being emphasized. Some will feel right at home using "invented" spelling while others will be hesitant. When they know that they may be in several groups during the course of a week, they are more comfortable about their performance and don't worry about who's "best." All of your children will need additional practice on one aspect of reading or another, and you are building a safety net under their efforts.

Use the Big Book, too, to establish the concepts of "beginning" and "ending" of a book, of front, back, top, bottom, right and left, illustration, print, letters, spaces, words, sentences, capital letters, and later on, punctuation. Do not assume they know these concepts.

As follow-up activities, some teachers make sentence strips of Big Book sentences for matching purposes. Print two or three sentences on paper and make enough copies for each child in the group. Leave room between the sentences so the children can match them up underneath. Cut out the same two or three sentences and turn them over on a desk. Working in pairs or alone, the children select one sentence strip at a time and match it with the sentence on their papers.

As they progress, they can use that same paper with the sentences on it to create a matching sentence made of separate *words* from a word strip collection. They are manipulating word cards and sentence parts into a sentence sequence that makes sense based on familiar materials.

At the same time you are giving your children this intensive study of one Big Book, you are also reading aloud from many other books they enjoy, and discussing them in a whole class setting. These books can be left on tables or in the book corner for further reading and enjoyment.

As they learn letter names, letter forms, and letter/sound correspondences, some of the children will begin to pick out words they recognize or can predict from what they have heard. It is most important to use books with rich language, fast-moving plots, and helpful illustrations to give them the support they need in their discoveries about surface print structure.

The seventh day

When a Big Book has been thoroughly read and understood, tell the children that you are going to give them their own individual copies of that book. Ask them to read their small copies aloud with you as you read from the Big Book. Then suggest that they read aloud to each other, in pairs, so that they get a second reading and can become used to their own copies. These small editions become references for their own writing, and for illustration ideas.

The children should perceive this as a kind of "graduation" time for them. They know that you believe they can "read" that book all by themselves and you're proud of their accomplishment. This is a happy time for them. They will read the small copies to themselves, to each other, to anyone who will listen to them! They have achieved something quite exceptional and need to have as much gratifying praise as possible. Some schools permit children to take home these small editions of the Big Books and read them to a second audience for even more praise. You can have the children read aloud to you individually, away from the group, before they take the copies home, just to be sure they have absorbed enough of the deep structure to be able to "read" it without embarrassment.

If you have a tape recorder available, you and your children can make your own tape of the book, dividing it up into sections so that everyone participates. In this way the tape is representative of the whole group's achievement.

If tape recorders are available only to older students, you and your children might consider asking a fifth- or sixth-grade teacher and class for help. Upper-grade teachers often have students who will profit from some additional print processing. The older students decide on voices for the taping and read the book. Some intermediate classes add simple sound effects to please the younger children. Your group can compose a letter asking for help and then decide on a suitable thank-you for the help they receive. They could:

- write a thank-you letter
- paint a thank-you picture
- make a thank-you collage
- memorize a thank-you poem

Your children can also share the smaller versions of the Big Book among themselves, using them as references when they want a word or phrase for their personal writing. Some of the Big Books can easily become short plays, with dialogue taken right from the books. Children can also make tongue-depressor puppets of the characters in the Big Books. They draw the characters, color them, cut them out and paste them on the top half of tongue depressors. Then they turn over a desk and use it as a stage for their impromptu puppet show, with dialogue made up from the stories.

Some advance planning suggestions

How to start each day

Just as athletes and singers need warm-ups, so do children. Begin each day as a whole class with one or more chants, songs, poems, or rhymes. Sing or recite the selections first and then have the children join in with you. This is a "ready-to-go" activity and children enjoy it, especially if you draw the parallel between their reading warm-ups and athletes' warm-up activities.

As it becomes clear what their favorites are, repeat those regularly. Put the short ones on chart paper so the children can see what they are singing and saying. Use them in group sessions, moving your finger or pointer under each word. You are helping them to "match" the words they know with the words as they appear in print. Because they are reading aloud together, they will self-correct as they go along.

Sometimes you might put a written chant or rhyme on the board or on chart paper *without* reading it aloud first. Your children have become risk-takers and will enjoy the opportunity to test their learning strategies on unknown materials. The rhyming words will help them succeed.

How to store and distribute Big Books

Each new Big Book should be a joint new adventure. It is crucial that your children's first encounter with the story be an "event," full of satisfaction, pleasure and meaning. Only *you* can ensure all that at this stage, so keep the Big Books off to one side until you're ready to present them. You can use a broad shelf or the boxes they came in. Stores that sell posters have handy storage cases and might give or sell one to you.

What to do about the other groups

Almost inevitably when you begin reading a Big Book with one group, the other children will have their ears "extended" so they won't miss a bit of the excitement. And that's fine. After a short time, many of them will give up trying to hear and go back to the work that's been generated from their own reading and discussions: writing stories, painting, copying, puppet-making, taping, and reading from small editions. If a few children do want to hear everything, let them. They'll be just that much more enthusiastic when their time comes!

How to form groups

Groups are always temporary. Your first groups may even be quite random because you'll want to see how each of your children is constructing language. You'll need to see each child frequently in those beginning weeks, so each should participate in *many* groups. As you begin to sort them out, recognizing those who can move on and those who will need more time, you'll refine your groups. But you'll keep them flexible, moving individual children as a subject is tackled that will be especially interesting to one, as a demonstration comes up that will be useful to another, as one or two children ask to share with a special friend once in a while. Also a good deal of work will be done with the whole class, as you teach strategies every child needs to know.

When to do group work

Reading and writing go on all day long, as do speaking and listening, but you may want to set aside specific time for Big Books (and predictable books — see pages 28-29). Children appreciate order and consistency. They like to know what's coming next and they will feel comfortable when they know what they are doing each morning when they come into class. Many teachers prefer to have their children do any intensive learning early in the morning.

How to save time

Make a *What-to-Do* chart. You and your children decide what is to be done when emergencies arise during group reading time. Decide what to do when a pencil breaks, when more paper is needed, when a paint jar needs opening, when a word needs to be identified. What will happen when someone is not feeling well, when one child absolutely needs the teacher's attention, when a tape is needed for the cassette player, or when a child needs a new book? Discuss procedures and make a chart with the necessary "reminder" words. Children appreciate knowing what is correct because they want to do what's right.

How to use a read-aloud service

Older boys and girls in the school are tremendous sources for reading aloud to young children. They find and read books, often at specific times of each day, and the benefits are tremendous for both. A *Read-Aloud Service* can be set up with another teacher, and older boys and girls can sign up to read a book, tell a story, act out a playlet, read some poems, or just listen to the younger children read!

How to help parents

It is always prudent to let your parents know what their children are doing before the books go home. Make sure they understand that their children are using *both* memory (memory of the story structure) *and* the meaning of the words, the syntax of the sentences, and the graphophonic information to arrive at meaning. Alert your parents to the fact that their children will switch from "saying" the book to actually reading some words slowly and carefully, and that this is perfectly natural.

It is often helpful for parents to realize that what you are doing is the same as what they did when their children were learning how to talk. As their children's first teachers, they taught them how to use the language orally, accepting miscues and approximations, just as you do as they learn to read. They got the gist of what their children were saying, the deep structure, and *then* helped with the surface structure, with correct words, and syntax. That's exactly the approach you are using as well.

What to do with predictable books

Predictable books are easy to remember and read. Many are old folktales and rhymes. These were *told*, not read, and the audience needed to hear events and patterns repeated in order to follow the story. Predictable books are solid, quality children's books, and many of them have long been part of the repertoire of children's literature. Just look at the list at the end of the book — I'll be surprised if you don't know most of them already!

Why are they called "predictable books"? The reason is simple. Over the past few years we have discovered (rediscovered?) that many of the old favorites have the precise features that help children to more easily cope with text! They have any or all of the following:

- rhythm
- rhyme
- repetition of vocabulary
- repetition of story structure
- common story patterns (some call these "the grammar of a story")

If your children have read some Big Books and their smaller editions, they have internalized the shared-reading pattern and will be ready to read predictable books in the same way. Display them so as to invite the children to pick them up and read them. (You should have enough copies for yourself and each member of the group.)

The first day

Before you give the children their copies, do just what you did when you introduced the Big Books. Show them the cover, passing your copy around the group so each member can have a good look. Then ask, "What do you see?" Keep track of their observations on chart paper or the chalkboard, and put the child's initial beside each observation. Then ask, "What do you think we'll read about in this story?" Give them time to predict what might happen in the story and what questions the story might answer. Keep a record of these responses as well, a cooperative databank of observations.

Read the book aloud all the way through, with enthusiasm and all the "ham" you can muster. When you have finished, check the predictions to see how many were close. Have the children find their own responses and initials. Read them aloud and decide which ones have been confirmed by the story.

The second day

Read the story aloud again, pausing for comments and questions on each page as you read. Then read it once more, inviting the children to join in whenever they think they can predict what words are coming up next. Finally, read the story a third time, pausing before repetitive parts so the children can join in, independently, in oral cloze.

The third day

Use written cloze. Put two or three sentences from the book on the chalkboard, with one word deleted from each. Read each sentence aloud, using the word "something" as a placeholder for the deleted word. Ask the children to rerun the sentence to predict what the word might be. Have one child come to the board and read the sentence, pointing to each word as it is read, and reading the predicted word at the placeholder spot. Encourage the children to discuss the deleted word and suggest alternate words that might also fit the sentence.

Start with a long line to indicate a deletion. As your children become more adept at recognizing words and letter clusters, give them letter blanks instead, to indicate how many letters are in the missing word.

Some children enjoy finding a "cloze sentence" in their own independent reading to bring to the group. They tell you ahead of time what word they want deleted, and bring their book to the group. Then they watch the rest of the group making educated guesses about their sentences and reading aloud from their book.

The fourth day

Give the children their own copies of the predictable book and allow them time to go over it together. They can look more closely at the illustrations, find a word or two they already know, and verify what they've learned. Invite them to read along, aloud, from their own copies as you read the story one more time. Suggest that they run their fingers underneath the words so they can follow along more easily.

This is a good time for you to watch your children carefully to see which ones are "matching up" the printed words with their voices. This eye/voice matching occurs at different times for different children. Some may be trying to focus on each word as they read it aloud, while others may still be "saying" much of the story, reading from their memory of the deep structure without focusing on and matching their spoken words with the printed ones. The "saying" children can become part of another group that needs extra time to hear and share stories, to find words and phrases they recognize. Often these children have not heard enough bedtime stories in their lives, and have not come to school already familiar with books and book language. They need extra time to explore print and find out how it works.

The fifth day

Show-off day! As you and your children are reading the story aloud together, stop just before a repetitive section and ask a child you *know* can read it to do so for the group. Ask another child to read the same section or another similar one, as the others follow along. Children need a time to display their abilities, to validate what they've learned, and to be praised by you and their peers.

Predictable patterns

After you have completed five days with a predictable book, there is a second way you may want to use it, one that makes further use of the "story grammar."

There are simple patterns to be found in predictable stories. Three of the most familiar are:

- cause and effect
- problem and solution
- lists and sequences

Some books will have more than one pattern, and can be used again to discuss a second one.

Cause and effect

This pattern is not easy for young children to identify. They understand cause and effect once the pattern is made clear, but they often have trouble finding it independently.

In *The Magic Fish*, the fisherman's wife is so greedy that she loses all the gifts given to them by the magic fish.

20

In *Seven Little Rabbits,* the procession calling on old friend toad keeps getting smaller and smaller as each little rabbit becomes tired and drops off to sleep in the mole's home.

The Rose in My Garden presents an ever-widening picture of a serene garden that is abruptly shattered when the cat with the tattered ear chases the fieldmouse and wakes up the rose that begins the story.

Problem and solution

In *Stone Soup,* the young man solves his problem of hunger by persuading an old lady to make soup for him, using a stone as the base.

The same pattern appears in *Doctor De Soto,* where the dentist has to figure out how to help a fox without being eaten by him.

Clifford, in *Clifford's Family,* is an excellent problem solver. He removes a taxi that's blocking a crosswalk, provides an escape route during a fire, and jumps out of the way of a bull.

Noisy Nora tells about a middle mouse who can't get any attention from the rest of the family. She solves the problem by hiding and causing everyone to hunt for her.

Lists and sequences

A cumulative pattern is often used in children's literature.

In *A Rose in My Garden,* the author starts off with just the rose and widens his description to include many other plants and creatures.

Stone Soup has a growing accumulation of items going into the soup. The list is repeated each time a new item is added.

Over in the Meadow uses mothers and babies to show growing family size.

The following are suggestions for working with story patterns, to be used *after* your children are thoroughly familiar with the books. When they have heard and read ten or twelve books, the children can be helped to isolate and identify some of the patterns they have absorbed.

As your children are reading and listening to stories, point out the patterns and urge them to anticipate and predict what is coming next. They do this *unconsciously* and *intuitively* to an extent, but when you point the patterns out, you are helping them to articulate what they already know, and to use that knowledge deliberately when they read new books and when they do their own writing.

Cause and effect

If your children have read *Noisy Nora*, they have no doubt already talked about what caused Nora to do all the things she did. Perhaps they have also talked about what else she might have done to let her family know she was unhappy. Ask the children why she was unhappy and what she did because she was unhappy. Help them to articulate the *cause* (members of the family were so busy with other things that they forgot about her) and the *effect* (she got their attention!). Put two boxes on the board labeled *Cause* and *Effect*. Point out to the children that "cause" is *what makes something happen* and "effect" is *what happens,* and use a few words under each heading as reminders of the story.

Remind the children, too, that "cause" is in a word they know very well: "because." As they are examining the cause and effect pattern in their stories, ask them to make a mental note of how many times they hear the word "because" during a morning. They can set aside a piece of paper to keep track, if they like, and perhaps write a word or two to remember by. Later they can share their experiences with the whole class. (When all of your children have heard all of the books, it saves time and makes sense to discuss story patterns with the whole class.)

Briefly hold up two or three other familiar books and refresh their memories about each one. Focus on the pattern. What caused what to happen? Put the titles on the board. Make two boxes for each title, one for cause and one for effect.

Next ask the children to think of other books they know. Can they generalize to their own independent reading? Can they remember causes and effects from those books? This experience would be greatly enriched if you were to read aloud to the whole class some of the books the children remember.

As you continue to read new books, ask your children to watch for the cause/effect pattern. As they write their own stories, suggest that they make sure their readers will understand causes and effects. As a further help, suggest that they write a letter to the principal asking him to visit and tell them what "caused" him to become a principal. Other members of the community could be invited too.

Children ask "why" all the time. Take advantage of their natural curiosity by putting some effects on the board and asking them to generate some ideas about causes. For instance, you might draw a cracked vase on the chalkboard. Ask the children to speculate about what caused the damage. Add a table underneath and a cat beside. Now ask for the cause again. Put the words "cause" and "effect" next to the appropriate notes on the chalkboard.

Some children might like to draw pairs of cause/effect pictures. Remind them of some causes and effects they are familiar with:

- What happens when they forget their lunch or their milk money?
- What happens when there is sunshine in the morning and rain when they leave school in the afternoon?
- What happens when they drop a book in a puddle on the street?

You might suggest that they ask their parents to tell them about a specific occasion when they did something that made their parents very happy, and report to the class.

Before the children arrive in the morning, turn a chair over in the middle of the floor. Ask them to imagine the most outrageous thing that could have caused the upside-down chair. A dinosaur? A clown? A flood during the night? An army of ants? The group might like to write a cooperative story about their wonderful ideas.

Problem and solution

Children know a lot about problems. As an introduction to this story pattern, you might ask them what large or small problems they've had in the last two days. Give them time to talk about their problems and what they did about them. Put a problem box and a solution box on the board and fill them in with their suggestions. Discuss the problems and consider the solutions that took place or that might have taken place.

Ask your children if they have heard or read any books where the main character had a problem. Some will already have read *Noisy Nora*, and will remember that she had a problem with her family: she couldn't get anyone's attention and had to resort to extreme measures to have them notice her. They may also remember that in *Doctor De Soto* the doctor had to find a way to help the fox without becoming his dinner. Some of them may remember *Stone Soup*, in which the young man had to find a way to get something to eat.

Read several problem books aloud and ask the children to identify the problem and the solution. Consult the list on pages 28-29 for suggestions.

On another day ask your children to think about a school problem. After a day or so to think about it, have them interview each other to learn what each one thinks is the most important problem in the school. When the list of problems is completed, the whole group can identify the two most urgent ones and talk about possible solutions. You might involve another classroom as well, and continue the discussion until some solutions are clear enough to be presented to the principal.

If your children can take brief notes, you might have them interview an adult to find out what that person thinks is the most serious problem in the world today. You have been summarizing problems and solutions for them. Now they can try doing that on their own. Again the results of their findings can be shared with other classes, in posters or collages, for instance.

As they continue their independent reading, the children can identify problems and solutions that arise in books and can draw on their own personal experiences for parallels. In this way you are creating a climate for a safe exchange of ideas about problems that come up in your children's lives. You are giving them a format and a vocabulary to use, and they will feel more comfortable with and open about their difficulties.

Lists and sequences

One of the earliest patterns children use in their writing and speaking involves the connective "and." They talk and write in lists and sequences, stringing events together with "and" to keep stories going. As they become familiar with the shapes of sentences, with capital letters, periods and question marks, they will eliminate some of the "ands" in their writing, but will still use them in their speech.

Books that list things or events in sequence are loved by young children because once they hear the story they know what's going to happen next, and the pattern is an easy one to remember. There is a certain stability in these books that make them favorites. *Old MacDonald Had a Farm, The Gingerbread Man, I Know an Old Lady, Over in the Meadow, Chicken Soup with Rice, On Market Street, A Rose in My Garden, Seven Little Rabbits, Bunches and Bunches of Bunnies, Each Peach Pear Plum,* and *The New Baby Calf* have well defined sequences, and some of them have rhymes as well, making them even easier to remember.

Start out by demonstrating what a list is, and a sequence. Ask one child to tell you what he or she does in the morning *after* dressing for school and *before* going out the door. This limited time frame makes it easier for children to remember and to put their activities into a sequence. List the child's activities on the chalkboard and then ask for other similar sequences from other children. How do the sequences differ? Some of your children may have chores to do before going to school, some may take care of a pet, some may help a younger member of the family get ready for school or eat breakfast. Some lists may contain the same activities but in a different order. Explain that what they have done is to construct a list and a sequence of activities *in time*.

On another day ask them to think about other occasions when they or adults make lists. Some of them may suggest grocery lists, lists of things to take on a holiday, lists of "things to do" made by adults to help themselves to remember tasks. Some may have made lists of people to invite to a birthday party or of things to do to prepare for one.

Explain that things happen in sequence in books too. You've been using the words *beginning* and *end* or *ending* as you've been working on the graphophonic strategy. Use those words again when you ask your children to remember what happened at the beginning of a story and what happened at the end. This is a good time to refresh their memories about the words *first, next* and *last*. (Most folktales have three major events because three was about the limit a storyteller's audience could remember while listening to a story.) Put those sequence words on the board so the children can see them as the say them. Read or reread one of the list/sequence books suggested on pages 28-29 and ask the children what happened first, next and last. If there are a lot of items in a list, such as in *A Rose in My Garden*, make a game of remembering *some* of the items.

Sometimes books are organized around a different list or sequence basis: an alphabet *(On Market Street)*, months of the year *(Chicken Soup with Rice)*, numbers *(Seven Little Rabbits)*, parts of the whole *(Each Peach Pear Plum)*. As you are rereading books, point out the variety of ways in which lists and sequences can be organized.

The Little Red Hen is an especially good book for recalling events in sequence because each event is accompanied by a repetitive segment of the story, and the events follow a natural pattern of growth and activity. As they are hearing and reading this book, you might ask your children to bring in a favorite bread or cake recipe from home and make a cookbook for everyone to share. This can also be done with *Stone Soup*.

As the children remember what went into the soup, ask them about their own favorite soups and include those in a soup cookbook.

On another day ask your children to remember their favorite day. Give them time to choose a day and time to talk about what they did that day. List on the chalkboard the activities of the first few children, with their initials at the end of their lists. You won't be able to get to everyone's favorite day right away, but later you might take their dictation so they can have a record of that particular day. The first few children can copy their favorite day details from the board. These compositions are good ones to share with parents.

If the school nurse is available, your children might like to hear what a school nurse's day is like — or the principal's, or the dietician's, or any adult's who would be available and willing to share a typical day with them. (A guest is always an opportunity for learning and writing: the invitation, the questions, the thank-you note.)

There are more than these three patterns in children's books, of course, but these three are the most common and can easily be used by the children themselves. In their own writing, they can describe a problem and its solution, create a story that explains the "because," or help their readers remember stories by organizing the ideas and information in a list or sequence.

Conclusion

Big Books and predictable books allow your children to role-play themselves as successful readers right from the start! Their use provides "competency motivation." Children learn because they know they *can* learn, and they want to read because they believe they *can* read. And with such books, they *can!*

They learn to look for meaning in print, to rerun a sentence for semantic and syntactic validity, to predict and confirm routinely, and to self-correct when something doesn't sound right. They become risk-takers. They will try a new book without hesitation. And the safety net you build under their efforts will hold.

More importantly, their confidence allows them to generate their own learning projects. Your classroom will truly become a cooperative, self-generating and regenerating learning community.

Big Books from Scholastic
Boss for a Week
Bunches and Bunches of Bunnies
Cats and Mice
Clifford's Family
Have You Seen Birds?
A House Is a House for Me
Jump, Frog, Jump
The Little Red Hen
More Spaghetti, I Say!
The New Baby Calf
Noisy Nora
On Market Street
The Owl and the Pussycat
There Are Trolls
Where Have You Been?
Why Can't I Fly?
Wynken, Blynken and Nod

In preparation
All the Pretty Horses
The Bremen-Town Musicians
How Much Is a Million?
The Three Billy Goats Gruff

Predictable books from Scholastic
C/E Cause and effect books
P/S Problem and solution books
L/S List and sequence books

The Adventures of the Three Blind Mice C/E,P/S
Birthday Yo-Yo P/S
Boss for a Week L/S,P/S
Bremen-Town Musicians C/E,L/S
Bunches and Bunches of Bunnies L/S
The Carrot Seed C/E,L/S
Cats and Mice C/E
Chicken Soup with Rice L/S
Clifford's Family P/S
Days with Frog and Toad C/E,P/S
Doctor De Soto P/S

The Elves and the Shoemaker C/E
The Emperor's New Clothes C/E,P/S
Frog and Toad Are Friends C/E,P/S
Frog and Toad Together C/E,P/S
Frog Went A-Courtin' L/S
The Gingerbread Man C/E,P/S
Henny Penny C/E
How to Get Rid of Bad Dreams P/S
I Know an Old Lady L/S
I Was Walking Down the Road C/E,L/S
In My Back Yard L/S
Jump, Frog, Jump C/E,L/S
Just in Time for the King's Birthday C/E,L/S
The Lilly Pilly Tree C/E,P/S
The Little Red Hen C/E
The Magic Fish C/E
The Mitten C/E,P/S,L/S
More Spaghetti, I Say! C/E
The New Baby Calf L/S
Nice New Neighbors C/E,P/S
Noisy Nora C/E,P/S
Old MacDonald Had a Farm L/S
On Market Street C/E,L/S
Oops! P/S
Over in the Meadow L/S
The Rose in My Garden C/E,L/S
Seven Little Rabbits C/E
Six Foolish Fishermen C/E
Something Absolutely Enormous C/E
Stone Soup P/S,L/S
There Are Trolls C/E
The Three Bears C/E
The Three Billy Goats Gruff C/E,P/S
Three Ducks Went Wandering C/E
Tikki Tikki Tembo C/E,P/S
The Very Hungry Caterpillar C/E,L/S
Where Have You Been? L/S
Why Can't I Fly? P/S
Wind C/E
Wynken, Blynken and Nod L/S

Titles in the New Directions series

Each book in the New Directions series deals with a single, practical classroom topic or concern, teaching strategy or approach. Many teachers have recognized the collegial and encouraging tone in them — not surprising, since most of them have been written by practicing teachers. Indeed, if you have an idea for a New Directions title of your own, we encourage you to contact the Publishing Division, Scholastic Canada Ltd.

Existing titles include:

In Canada, order from: Scholastic Canada Ltd.,
123 Newkirk Road, Richmond Hill, ON L4C 3G5

In the United States, order from: Scholastic Inc., Box 7502,
Jefferson City, MO 65102